Introduction to Bible Origin

A Study of the Formation of the Bible

"The entrance of your words gives light."
–Psalm 119:130

Introduction to Bible Origin

A Study of the Formation of the Bible

Dr. S. Walker

Introduction to Bible Origin
Copyright © 2003 by Sheila Walker
ISBN 0-9724220-1-3

Published by:
Sheila Walker
S. Walker Publications
P. O. Box 164048
Orlando, FL 32716
www.swalkerpublications.com

Printed in the United States of America

Cover Photo: Dr. S. Walker

Volume 1: Introduction to Bible Doctrine
    A Systematic Study of Seven Doctrines of the Christian Faith—Made Easy
Volume 2: Introduction to Bible Origin
    A Study of the Formation of the Bible
Volume 3: Introduction to Typology and Symbolism
    An Expository Study of Types and Symbols Found in the Bible

CONTENTS

Introduction to Bible Origin gives an overview of how the Bible came into existence. This study focuses on how the writings came about, through revelation and inspiration. It will assist in understanding why the books of the Christian Bible are deemed as having divine authority.

The Bible should be read at least once within every man's lifetime because it reveals God's plan, purpose and will for him. It relates to man's life and destiny. If these facts are so, then one should understand how the Bible came to be as well as understand the method of the author . . . God, who wrote through human hands.

"The entrance of your words gives light."
Psalm 119:130

CHAPTER 1

REVELATION AND INSPIRATION

How God spoke to man has been a topic of great interest throughout the centuries. Man has often wondered how God made Himself known. Though man has the Bible, he is naturally curious as to how it came about and what authorizes it to be divine truth.

The Bible speaks of *revelation* as a method God uses to make Himself known. God reveals Himself and imparts knowledge so that man becomes aware of the reality of God.

Ephesians 3:1–3 "For this reason, I, Paul, the prisoner of Christ Jesus for the sake of you Gentiles—if indeed you have heard of the stewardship of God's grace which was given to me for you; that by revelation there was made known to me the mystery, as I wrote before in brief."

1st Corinthians 14:6 "But now, brethren, if I come to you speaking in tongues, what shall I profit you, unless I speak to you either by way of revelation or of knowledge or of prophecy or of teaching?"

There are three variations of the revelation of God in the Bible: *dreams, visions, and direct communication.*

Dreams are revelations of God that are given during sleep.[1] Because one's own imaginations and emotions are transmitted through the mind while asleep, dreams can be easily misinterpreted as being revelations from God.[2] This is primarily the reason dreams are considered the lower form of God's revelation.

Genesis 20:3 "But God came to Abimelech in a dream of the night, and said to him, 'Behold, you are a dead man because of the woman whom you have taken, for she is married.'"

Genesis 31:24 "And God came to Laban the Aramean in a dream of the night, and said to him, 'Be careful that you do not speak to Jacob either good or bad.'"

Visions are very close to what is called "trance."

In this experience the revelation of God is extremely vivid. While the person is awake they are conscious of divine impartation.[3]

Acts 7:54–56 "Now when they heard this, they were cut to the quick, and they began gnashing their teeth at him. But being full of the Holy Spirit, he gazed intently into heaven and saw the glory of God, and Jesus

---

1. *1st Kings 3:5.* 2. *Deuteronomy 13:1–3.* 3. *Acts 10:1–6*

standing at the right hand of God; and he said, 'Behold, I see the heavens opened up and the Son of Man standing at the right hand of God.'"

Acts 10:9–15 "And on the next day, as they were on their way, and approaching the city, Peter went up on the housetop about the sixth hour to pray. And he became hungry, and was desiring to eat; but while they were making preparations, he fell into a trance; and he beheld the sky opened up, and a certain object like a great sheet coming down, lowered by four corners to the ground, and there were in it all kinds of four-footed animals and crawling creatures of the earth and birds of the air. And a voice came to him, 'Arise, Peter, kill and eat!' But Peter said, 'By no means, Lord, for I have never eaten anything unholy and unclean.' And again a voice came to him a second time, 'What God has cleansed, no longer consider unholy.' And this happened three times; and immediately the object was taken up into the sky."

Direct Communication is the highest form of revelation. In the Bible, the revelation of God is given to individuals who are neither asleep or in a trance. The revelation of God is actually spoken to a person who is in a state of consciousness.[4] In some cases of this type of revelation, the appearance of God[5] was also experienced.

Genesis 26:1–4 "Now there was a famine in the land, besides the previous famine that had occurred in the days of Abraham. So Isaac went to Gerar, to Abimelech king of the Philistines. And the LORD appeared to him and said, 'Do not go down to Egypt; stay in the land of which I shall tell you. Sojourn in this land and I will be with you and bless you, for to you and to your descendants I will give all these lands, and I will establish the oath which I swore to your father Abraham. And I will multiply your descendants as the stars of heaven, and will give your descendants all these lands; and by your descendants all the nations of the earth shall be blessed.'"

Exodus 3:3–6 "So Moses said, 'I must turn aside now, and see this marvelous sight, why the bush is not burned up.' When the LORD saw that he turned aside to look, God called to him from the midst of the bush, and said, 'Moses, Moses!' And he said, 'Here I am.' Then He said, 'Do not come near here; remove your sandals from your feet, for the place on which you are standing is holy ground.' He said also, 'I am the God of your father, the God of Abraham, the God of Isaac, and the God of Jacob.' Then Moses hid his face, for he was afraid to look at God."

Acts 9:1–6 "Now Saul, still breathing threats and murder against the disciples of the Lord, went to the high priest, and asked for letters from him to the synagogues at Damascus, so that if he found any belonging to the Way, both men and women, he might bring them bound to Jerusalem. And it came about that as he journeyed, he was approaching Damascus, and suddenly a light from heaven flashed around him; and he fell to

---

4. *Amos 9:1, Isaiah 6:1–8.*   5. *In most experiences the sight of God was a Theophany (the appearance of God in angelic or human form).*

the ground, and heard a voice saying to him, 'Saul, Saul, why are you persecuting Me?' And he said, 'Who art Thou, Lord?' And He said, 'I am Jesus whom you are persecuting, but rise, and enter the city, and it shall be told you what you must do.'"

There are two phases involved in the revelation of God: *receiving and responding*.

What we've just discussed is the receiving phase of the revelation of God. Responding to God's revelation is known as *inspiration*. Inspiration is divine guidance that gives understanding to the recipient. This authenticates the revelation of God from mere human thought. In writing the Bible the Holy Spirit led and directed the inspiration of its human authors. This inspiration is considered the infusion of the breath of God into the writing of the Scriptures. The inspiration of God and directing of the Holy Spirit is what gives the Scriptures divine authority, distinguishing the writings from human thoughts.

Job 32:8 "But it is a spirit in man, And the breath of the Almighty gives them understanding."

2nd Timothy 3:16 "All Scripture is inspired by God and profitable for teaching, for reproof, for correction, for training in righteousness."

2nd Peter 1:19–21 "And so we have the prophetic word made more sure, to which you do well to pay attention as to a lamp shining in a dark place, until the day dawns and the morning star arises in your hearts. But know this first of all, that no prophecy of Scriptures is a matter of one's own interpretation, for no prophecy was ever made by an act of human will, but men moved by the Holy Spirit spoke from God." ❖

NOTES

CHAPTER 2

THE OLD TESTAMENT

The Hebrew Bible Jesus used was divided into three sections: *The Law, The Prophets, and The Writings.*[6]

Luke 24:44 "Now He said to them, 'These are My words which I spoke to you while I was still with you, that all things which are written about Me in the Law of Moses and the Prophets and the Psalms must be fulfilled.'"

In the New Testament, Jesus refers to the Old Testament in several ways. He defines it as:

The Law

Matthew 5:18 "For truly I say to you, until heaven and earth pass away, not the smallest letter or stroke shall pass away from the Law, until all is accomplished."

The Law and The Prophets

Matthew 7:12 "Therefore, however you want people to treat you, so treat them, for this is the Law and the Prophets."

Moses and the Prophets

Luke 16:31 "But He said to him, 'If they do not listen to Moses and the Prophets, neither will they be persuaded if someone rises from the dead.'"

SECTION ONE
THE LAW

The first five books of the Old Testament are referred to as *The Five Books of Moses, The Torah,*[7] *and The Pentateuch.*[8]

Since the Bible gives no details, the work of archeologists has answered many questions on how Moses obtained the information for his narratives about creation, the fall and the deluge, which occurred before his birth. The findings of Babylonian and Assyrian accounts prove that all of these events actually took place. Their documentation of these events is very similar to that of Moses. The major difference is that Moses transcends the involvement of one God in these events (*Monotheism*)[9] rather than the activity of "many gods" (*Polytheism*) as seen in the other accounts.

---

6. *The Writings are also called The Sacred Writings or The Psalms.*   7. *Torah—in Hebrew means Law. It applies to divine law in the scriptures. Torah also means direction or instruction.*   8. *Pentateuch—(pen'ta'took) meaning "five fold books" in Greek.*   9. *Monotheism—the worship of "one god." Polytheism—the worship of "many gods."*

Writing

Archeological finds prove that the art of writing existed in early civilizations. Early culture gives many clues as to how some of the written sources were developed. Ur, located on the banks of the Euphrates River, was a seaport for the city of Babylon. In the days of Abraham, this was a very wealthy civilization. The high standard of living, which was influenced by heavy trading and commerce, made record keeping necessary.

Abraham was raised in Ur and later moved to Haran, another trade civilization located in Canaan. The environments of these cities, as well as the migration of Abraham's family, played a great role in the recording of early biblical history.

Genesis 11:27–31 "Now these are the records of the generations of Terah. Terah became the father of Abram, Nahor and Haran; and Haran became the father of Lot. And Haran died in the presence of his father Terah in the land of his birth, in Ur of the Chaldeans. And Abram and Nahor took wives for themselves. The name of Abram's wife was Sarai; and the name of Nahor's wife was Milcah, the daughter of Haran, the father of Milcah and Iscah. And Sarai was barren; she had no child. And Terah took Abram his son, and Lot the son of Haran, his grandson, and Sarai his daughter-in-law, his son Abram's wife; and they went out together from Ur of the Chaldeans in order to enter the land of Canaan; and they went as far as Haran, and settled there."

Oral Tradition

It is human nature for man to pass information along verbally. There is no doubt that oral traditions and storytelling were means by which historical events passed from one generation to another. It was customary among Jews to verbally reiterate the history, traditions and practices of their religion to preserve their unique identity and culture. The Talmud[10] and the Mishnah[11] hold the values of Judaism, and brings its practice to life.

Exodus 12:24–27 "And you shall observe this event as an ordinance for you and your children forever. And it will come about when you enter the land which the LORD will give you, as He has promised, that you shall observe this rite. And it will come about when your children will say to you, 'What does this rite mean to you?' that you shall say, 'It is a Passover sacrifice to the LORD who passed over the houses of the sons of Israel in Egypt when He smote the Egyptians, but spared our homes.'"

Egyptian Influence

The most prominent family in Egypt raised Moses. As the Pharaoh's grandson, Moses was privy to a privileged education and most likely studied

10. *The Talmud—(traditional law, instruction or directions) is known as the Jewish Book of Tradition.*
11. *The Mishnah—a section of the Talmud that contains a repetition of oral laws.*

government, law and the arts. His royal upbringing contributed greatly to his research and writing abilities.

Exodus 2:5–10 "Then the daughter of Pharaoh came down to bathe at the Nile, with her maidens walking alongside the Nile; and she saw the basket among the reeds and sent her maid, and she brought it to her. When she opened it, she saw the child, and behold, the boy was crying. And she had pity on him and said, 'This is one of the Hebrews' children.' Then his sister said to Pharaoh's daughter, 'Shall I go and call a nurse for you from the Hebrew women, that she may nurse the child for you?' And Pharaoh's daughter said to her, 'Go ahead.' So the girl went and called the child's mother. Then Pharaoh's daughter said to her, 'Take this child away and nurse him for me and I shall give you your wages.' So the woman took the child and nursed him. And the child grew, and she brought him to Pharaoh's daughter, and he became her son. And she named him Moses, and said, 'Because I drew him out of the water.'"

Inspiration

Moses undoubtedly used oral tradition and written records as sources for Genesis, where he accounts events that occurred before his time. This being true, the question is raised concerning spirituality and divine authority. Inspiration from God explains the entire concept of the divine authority of the Bible. The Holy Spirit inspired the authors of the Bible for God's purposes, regardless of their sources. Through them, God exalts Himself above other gods, He clarifies His involvement in human history and He gives understanding of His will for mankind. Unlike the other records of the events Moses writes of, which proved to be of human origin, God used Moses while under the influence of inspiration. Therefore, his account is divine and authoritative.

1st Corinthians 2:12–13 "Now we have received, not the spirit of the world, but the Spirit who is from God, that we might know the things freely given to us by God, which things we speak, not in words taught by human wisdom, but in those taught by the Spirit, combining spiritual thoughts with spiritual words."

The remaining four books of the Pentateuch (Exodus, Leviticus, Numbers and Deuteronomy) are relative to actual events which occurred during the life of Moses.

Deuteronomy 31:9 "So Moses wrote this law and gave it to the priests, the sons of Levi who carried the ark of the covenant of the LORD, and to all the elders of Israel."

Deuteronomy 29:29 "The secret things belong to the LORD our God, but the things revealed belong to us and our sons forever, that we may observe all the words of this law."

SURVEY OF THE BOOKS OF THE LAW
Moses is the Author

GENESIS

Message: Genesis is called "The Book of Beginnings" because in its chapters the answer to the question "how did it all begin?" is answered. Through its many stories we learn of God's unmerited favor toward man. The first names of Deity are given (Elohim, Jehovah and Adoni). The first four covenants between God and man are found in this book (Edemic, Adamic, Noahic and Abrahamic). We learn of many relationships, the most important being the relationship between God and man. Between the first verse and the last, we comprehend the great favor, provision and grace of God toward His creation. Not to be overlooked is man's fall and God's promise of the redeemer, Jesus Christ, who would ultimately change man's life if he only believes in Him.

EXODUS

Message: Exodus is the "book of redemption." In Exodus, God takes Israel out of Egyptian bondage. The story typifies redemption from sin. To be taken out of something signifies being taken into something else. God therefore took His people out of bondage to take them into a relationship with Him of fellowship, worship and service.

LEVITICUS

Message: The proper preparation for fellowship with God is holiness. In Leviticus, God who now dwells in the Tabernacle, tells the redeemed how to walk, worship and fellowship with Him. The book has its name because it mainly records the duties of the Levites who were priests.

NUMBERS

Message: Numbers follows through with God's divine order. The story of Israel's wilderness experience depicts the sovereignty of God. Service is the principal message of Numbers. Man being created in Genesis, redeemed in Exodus, given the correct order of fellowship and worship in Leviticus, is now numbered for service. Being separated unto God, everyone was designated to service; this was the purpose for cataloging Israel. The redeemed are saved to serve.

DEUTERONOMY

Message: Although the book of Deuteronomy reiterates the events, laws and history of Israel, its main purpose is to make the past applicable to the future. Moses attempts to prepare the chosen people of God to embark upon their inheritance. The method of preparation is simple; the people were to learn from past experiences. Israel's failures were due to a lack of faith, obedience and spirituality, which made it difficult to move ahead.

SECTION TWO
THE PROPHETS

The Prophets, a group of historical and prophetical writings, make up the second division of the Hebrew Bible.

The historical books are called the *Former Prophets,* they are: Joshua, Judges, 1st and 2nd Samuel (one book), 1st and 2nd Kings (one book). The fundamental message of these books is more moral and spiritual than they are historical.

The prophetical books are called the *Latter Prophets* and are composed of two classifications of prophets. Known distinctively as Major Prophets are Isaiah, Jeremiah and Ezekiel. Their messages resembled sermons that addressed the declension of Israel. Hosea, Joel, Amos, Obadiah, Jonah, Micah, Nahum, Habakkuk, Zephaniah, Haggai, Zechariah, and Malachi are known as the Twelve Minor Prophets, they also addressed the apostasy[12] and declension[13] of Israel in sermon style.

SURVEY OF THE FORMER PROPHETS
Various Authors

JOSHUA   *Author: The Talmud assigns*
                                authorship to Joshua

Message: Joshua became the successor of Moses. His challenging mission was to lead God's people into the Promised Land. With opposition and resistance, God's people were responsible for occupying what was rightfully theirs. The credit for Joshua's conquests is attributed to God's divine leadership.

JUDGES   *Author: Samuel*

Message: After the death of Joshua, Israel fell into a period of rebellion, declension and apostasy. The history of the struggles of the individual tribes to exist among foreigners with their ungodly influences, describes the continued grace of God toward Israel. The punishment for disobedience was suffering, but repentance led to deliverance, which demonstrates the love of God. The installment of the thirteen judges was necessary to lead God's people out of the hands of those who oppressed them. Installing judges played a great role in unifying Israel.

---

12. Apostasy—"a falling away." 13. Declension—"a downward trend." *During a time of declension and apostasy in Israel, the prophets spoke on God's behalf to revive the nation of Israel. Although these messages contain chastisement they also demonstrate the mercy of God to provide solutions to problems and extends an offer for restoration.*

1ˢᵀ AND 2ᴺᴰ SAMUEL   *Author: Samuel with contributions*
from Nathan and Gad

Message: In Samuel we see the line of writing prophets and the line of kings. Samuel records the establishment of monarchy in Israel as well as the overwhelming failure of the priesthood under Eli. Samuel was the last judge and the first prophet. Being a faithful and spiritual man who exhibited spiritual discernment, Samuel speaks from the prophetic office rather than the priest's office. Both books record the preservation of God's people. In these books, God prepared His people for what was to follow in the lineage of David.

1ˢᵀ AND 2ᴺᴰ KINGS   *Author: Unknown*

Message: Originally these books (which contains more history than messages) appeared as one book. They were separated into two volumes when they were translated from Hebrew into Greek. 1ˢᵗ Kings is divided into two parts. Part one recounts the rule of King Solomon and part two tells the history of Judah and Israel. Solomon and the prophet Elijah are characterized in this book. 2ⁿᵈ Kings is a sequel to 1ˢᵗ Kings. It concentrates on the history of the two kingdoms, Judah and Israel. Elijah, Elisha and other prominent Bible figures are portrayed.

SURVEY OF THE LATTER PROPHETS
MAJOR PROPHETS
The Prophets are the Authors

ISAIAH

Message: Isaiah is known as the prophet of redemption because of the book's Messianic contents. We see the advent, mission, work and person of Jesus Christ throughout the book of Isaiah. Isaiah has two main parts with a historical parenthesis[14] in between. The first part concerns itself mainly with the prophecies of denunciation or condemnation (chapters 1–35). The prophecies are against immorality and idolatry, first among God's people and then extended to the nations, the book ends with the blessing of God and gathering of Israel. The second main part of Isaiah is Messianic. It contains prophecies of Israel's deliverance and future glory. This portion of Isaiah correlates with the New Testament.

JEREMIAH

Message: The book of Jeremiah has the apostasy, idolatry and immorality of Judah as its background setting. Through the overwhelming conditions of his time, the prophet remained faithful in his ministry for over forty years. Despite personal persecution, Jeremiah saw his prophecies fulfilled.

---

14. *Historical Parenthesis—an insert of scriptures that are not in sequence with the others; parenthetic inclusions.*

Ezekiel

Message: Ezekiel was a priest and a prophet who, while in exile in Babylon, prophesied using illustrations to get his message across. As his name in Hebrew means "God strengthens" or "strengthened by God," so was his message of national restoration. His message reminded the people of God's covenant promise of blessings. He emphasizes the sovereignty of God. Ezekiel is a prophet called not just to speak to the Ten Tribes of Judah, but rather to the "whole house" of Israel.

Survey of the Latter Prophets
Minor Prophets
The Prophets are the Authors

Hosea

Message: The message of Hosea is one that compels God's people to repent. Conviction is preached in a style that is straightforward and illustrative. Israel is illustrated as the dishonored wife of Jehovah who has been cast aside. Israel, the adulterous wife (which in Hosea is the Ten Tribes of the Northern Kingdom) will undergo purification and be restored by grace.

Joel

Message: Joel, a prophet of the Southern Kingdom, warned Judah of the coming "Day of Judgement" of the LORD. The warning was for both Israel and the nations. The time of the forthcoming judgement would not compare to the present plague of locusts, from which the prophet begins his message. Only those who called upon the name of the Lord would be saved from the tribulation.

Amos

Message: Under the prosperity of the Northern Kingdom the impure form of religion existed. Amos, seeing this, speaks out loud and clear against social injustice. Amos warned the perpetrators of their lack of grief over their unjust behavior. God's alternative would be to vindicate His moral character, which was to be seen in His people. The "Day of the LORD"[15] would undoubtedly come. Amos' mission, stemming from the mercy of God, was to warn the people to repent. The consequence of refusal was destruction.

Obadiah

Message: In this short book, which consists of twenty-one verses, Obadiah delivers a message, which has virtually no hope for deliverance. The certain judgement of Edom is retribution. The ongoing feud between the two brothers, Esau and Jacob was carried through to their descendants. The

---

15. *The Day of The LORD refers to the finalization of God's Kingdom when the enemies of His people are brought down. It begins with the Second Coming of Christ and ends with all things becoming new. John 14:3, Titus 2:13, Revelation 21:1.*

animosity of the Edomites (Esau) was to the extent of forbidding Israel (Jacob), on their way to Canaan, passage through their land. The greater extreme was Edom's siding with the enemy against Israel.

JONAH

Message: The main theme of the book of Jonah is the universality of the grace of God. Commissioned to warn of judgement, the bigoted spirit of Jonah caused him to resist his duty. Jonah, who was a Jew, feared that the Gentiles would indeed repent and become recipients of God's grace. The story typifies Christ taking salvation to the Gentiles.

MICAH

Message: Micah addresses social ethics and true spirituality. He focuses on the sins of Judah and Israel, which contrast the true righteousness of God. In this sermon of judgement and pardon, Jehovah brings up a case. The court proceedings go on to predict judgement for the sins committed specifically those of the judges, priests and prophets. The settlement of the case would be divine pardon. The prophet's closing statement to the court is a prayer of God's promised salvation.

NAHUM

Message: Nahum brings another message to Nineveh, only this time it's one of destruction. Jonah, sent by God to the Gentile city, brought revival that nearly lasted a century. God now marked the people of Nineveh who returned to their destructive, immoral and defiant ways for destruction. In scripture, Nineveh speaks of Gentile religiosity, while Babylon speaks of the confusion of the Gentile political system.

HABAKKUK

Message: The prophet Habakkuk had a troubled heart over the unrecompensed violation of God's Law. He wanted to know why God allowed such without punishment. When God revealed His plan to use the Chaldeans as a chastening rod for Judah, Habakkuk became even more perplexed. How could God use the Chaldeans who were even more corrupt than Judah? Faith in God's answer and trusting God's pure goodness, infinite wisdom and omnipotent power was what satisfied the prophet. Waiting and relying on the plan of God has the prophet conclude in praise.

ZEPHANIAH

Message: During a time of what seemed to be revival in Judah (2nd Kings 22 & 23), Zephaniah places emphasis on judgement and restoration in the Day of the LORD. Obviously the revival was superficial. The prophet harshly describes the judgement of not only God's own people but the nations as well. The impact of the Day of the LORD will be universal, all will be judged. However, there is to be another side of the judgement. The righteous remnant[16] that survived will experience Kingdom blessings. Zephaniah is a contemporary of Jeremiah.

HAGGAI

Message: This post-exile prophet shared the responsibility of Zechariah and Malachi, which was to provoke the feeble remnant of Jews who returned to Jerusalem to finish rebuilding. They had started under Nehemiah and Ezra, but allowed personal affairs to stop them from completing the work. A series of stirring sermons to raise the builder's enthusiasm is contained in this book. The LORD is not pleased when we lay aside His work.

ZECHARIAH

Message: Haggai used exhortation to motivate the people to complete the rebuilding of Jerusalem, and Zechariah used encouragement as his method. He encouraged them with the anticipation of the future purpose of the Temple in regard to the Messiah. Zechariah has a number of biblical symbols within its contents and is highly Messianic.

MALACHI

Message: Malachi closes the Old Testament with the last prophecy. As did Zechariah and Haggai, Malachi prophesies to the remnant, which were in Jerusalem after the exile. It seems as though the people of God fell back into the situations that caused them their captivity. The messenger brings a message of God's love, the sinful state of His people and of the Day of the LORD. From this last prophecy of the Old Testament begins 400 years of silence.

SECTION THREE
THE WRITINGS

The Sacred Writings of the Hebrew Bible is comprised of the Poetical Books, The Five Rolls and Historical Books.

The first of the poetical books is Psalms, the lyrical or songbook of Israel. Proverbs and Job are literary in content. The Megilloth (five rolls) comprises the second division of this category. Songs of Solomon, Ruth, Lamentations, Ecclesiastes and Esther were presented in temple services in rolls, hence the name "Five Rolls." Included in this category is the book of Daniel, which is prophetical and historical, Ezra and Nehemiah, which was considered one book for a time, and Chronicles, which is more of a reference book.

---

16. *Remnant—the people of God who are able to overcome political and spiritual challenges and remain faithful to their religious convictions.*

SURVEY OF THE POETICAL BOOKS
Various Authors

PSALMS

Author: David with contributions from Moses, Asaph, Sons of Korah, Solomon, Heman and anonymous writers.

Message: Psalms is the inspired praise and prayer book of Israel. It consists of five books, which encompasses the emotions and experiences of human life. While the Psalms give emphasis on the law and faith in Jehovah, Christ the Messiah is seen in a great number of them.

PROVERBS

Author: Solomon, with contributions from Agur and King Lemuel.

Message: God's people are admonished to be wise. Wisdom is an attribute of godly character; therefore it is attained through the Spirit of God. Proverbs provides practical teachings in wisdom, which are necessary for daily Christian living.

JOB

Author: Unknown

Message: Job is a book of poetry that tells the story of a godly man who is tested with suffering. Though the subject matter is suffering and the question is "why," contentment comes from having faith in God.

SURVEY OF THE MEGILLOTH
"FIVE ROLLS"
Various Authors

SONGS OF SOLOMON

Author: Solomon

Message: Love and marriage, which is ordained by God, makes the pure and honest feelings between a couple spiritual.

RUTH

Author: The Talmud attributes the book to Samuel

Message: The book of Ruth is set in the period of Judges. It is a heartwarming story of faithfulness and commitment, which gains its reward from God. The union of Ruth and Boaz gives lineage to Christ. In this story we are taught of the Gentiles coming to love the true God. In Matthew, chapter one, Ruth is among the Gentile women whose names appear in the genealogy of Christ (Tamar and Rehab are the other two).

LAMENTATIONS

Author: Jeremiah

Message: In this book the promised judgement of God fell and left the

Holy City in ruin. The five lamentations of Jeremiah depict God's sorrow for the people He chastened.

ECCLESIASTES   *Author: The author is said to be Solomon*

Message: Vanity is emphasized in this book. In scripture vanity means "empty" as opposed to the modern day translation of foolish pride or conceit. The speaker here is a wise man who speaks of the vanity of a life that is apart from God. He deems life empty and fruitless. It is God who supplies the gifts and rewards of life. Reasoning over the issues of life is brought to a conclusion.

ESTHER   *Author: Unknown*

Message: Clearly the message in Esther is one of faith and courage in a time of great struggle and difficulty. Although His name is not mentioned, God is depicted as the source of strength and victory in this book.

SURVEY OF THE HISTORICAL BOOKS
Various Authors

DANIEL   *Author: Daniel*

Message: Daniel's ministry covers the entire seventy years of the Babylonian captivity. The thrust of his message was the "times of the Gentile[17]," a fitting message for people who were undergoing Gentile oppression. The time would come when the Messianic Kingdom of God would last forever. God's method of dreams and visions given and interpreted through Daniel served as clear warnings to the Gentiles. The dreams were also reminders to God's people that He ultimately controlled the affairs of man. Daniel was a captive in Babylon as was Ezekiel. Daniel's prophecy coincides with Revelation and is considered the apocalypse[18] of the Old Testament.

EZRA   *Author: The Talmud ascribes the authorship to Ezra*

Message: Ezra is the first of the post-captivity books, the others are: Nehemiah, Esther, Haggai, Zechariah and Malachi. Ezra deals with a small number of Jews who were willing to return to Palestine despite the hardship and poverty that presented itself. Though the decree of Cyrus allowed the return from exile for the Jews, the prosperity of Babylon was the choice of most of them. The small remnant, which returned to Jerusalem, began to lay the foundation for the rebuilding of the Temple. They failed due to prevailing hindrances. However, the opposition fell under the influence of the prophecies of Haggai and Zechariah, which brought revival to the remnant. Ezra was sent to teach and enforce the Jewish law.

---

17. *Times of The Gentile—Read Luke 21:24 and Romans 11:25.*   18. *Apocalypse—God's revelation of His secrets that pertain to His plans for end times and the future. The two apocalyptic books of the Bible that coincide are Daniel and Revelation.*

NEHEMIAH   *Author:* Nehemiah

Message: A man of prayer and dedication, Nehemiah invokes a spirit of determination to have the walls around Jerusalem rebuilt. This was accomplished in fifty-two days despite opposition. He influenced civil and moral restoration as well as spiritual, all of which were necessary to restore the called-out people of God. Ezra and Nehemiah were regarded for a time as one book.

1ST AND 2ND CHRONICLES   *Author:* Ezra

Message: Religious unity under pagan monarchy[19] is the reason for the Chronicles. Covering the same periods of time as Samuel and Kings, the Chronicles provide a spiritual history and a higher foundation for God's people. ❖

---

19. *Monarchy—a government that is ruled by a monarch (a king, queen or emperor). See The Monarchy of Israel on page 25.*

NOTES

CHAPTER 3

1. CHRISTIAN CANONIZATION *OF THE* OLD TESTAMENT

The Pentateuch

Genesis	Exodus	Leviticus
Numbers	Deuteronomy	

The Historical Books

Joshua	Judges	Ruth
1st and 2nd Samuel	1st and 2nd Kings	1st and 2nd Chronicles
Ezra	Nehemiah	Esther

The Poetical Books

Job	Psalms	Proverbs
Ecclesiastes	Song of Solomon	

The Prophetical Books

Five Major Prophets

Isaiah	Jeremiah	Lamentations
Ezekiel	Daniel	

The Prophetical Books

Twelve Minor Prophets

Hosea	Joel	Amos
Obadiah	Jonah	Micah
Nahum	Habakkuk	Zephaniah
Haggai	Zechariah	Malachi

Chart Instruction: *Please read chart from left to right.*

2. Hebrew Canonization *of the Old Testament*

The Law		
The Five Books of Moses	The Torah	The Pentateuch

The Prophetical Books		

Part One: Historical Books or "Former Prophets"

Joshua	Judges	1st and 2nd Samuel
2st and 2nd Kings		

Part Two: The Latter Prophet—Three "Major Prophets"

Isaiah	Jeremiah	Ezekiel

The Twelve or "Minor Prophets"

Hosea	Joel	Amos
Obadiah	Jonah	Micah
Nahum	Habakkuk	Zephaniah
Haggai	Zechariah	Malachi

The Sacred Writings		

Poetical Books

Psalms	Proverbs	Job

Megillothm or "Five Rolls"

Songs of Solomon	Ruth	Lamentations
Ecclesiastes	Esther	

Megillothm

Daniel	Ezra and Nehemiah	Chronicles

Chart Instruction: *Please read chart from left to right.*

3. THE JUDGES OF ISRAEL

Judges were mainly military leaders of the Hebrews who were oppressed and had fallen away from their religion. Because of this, these leaders also served as political and moral advisors. The period of judges over Israel falls between the death of Joshua and monarch leadership. Israel had thirteen judges.

OTHNIEL	CHAPTER 3:7–11
EHUD	CHAPTER 3:12–30
SHAMGAR	CHAPTER 3:31
DEBORAH AND BARAK	CHAPTERS 4–5
GIDEON	CHAPTERS 6–8
ABIMELECH	CHAPTER 9
TOLA	CHAPTER 10: 1–2
JAIR	CHAPTER 10:3–5
JEPHTHAH	CHAPTERS 10:6
IBZAN	CHAPTER 12:8–10
ELON	CHAPTER 12:11–12
ABDON	CHAPTER 12:13–15
SAMSON	CHAPTERS 13–16

4. MONARCHY OF ISRAEL

THE UNITED KINGDOM

SAUL
DAVID
SOLOMON

THE DIVIDED KINGDOM

ISRAEL	JUDAH
(THE TEN TRIBES)	(TWO TRIBES: JUDAH & BENJAMIN)
Capital: Samaria	*Capital: Jerusalem*
JEROBOAM 22	REHOBOAM 17
NADAB 2	ABIJAM 3
BAASHA 24	ASA 41
ELAH 2	JEHOSHAPHAT 25
ZIMRI 7	JEHORAM 8
OMRI 8	AHAZIAH 1
AHAB 22	ATHALIAH 6 (QUEEN)
AHAZIAH 2	JEHOASH 40
JEHORAM 12	AMAZIAH 29
JEHU 28	UZZIAH 52
JEHOAHAZ 17	JOTHAM 16
JEHOASH 16	AHAZ 16
JEROBOAM II 41	HEZEKIAH 29
ZACHARIAH 6 MONTHS	MANASSEH 55
SHALLUM 1 MONTH	AMON 2
MENAHEM 10	JOSIAH 31
PEKAHIAH 2	JEHOAHAZ 3 MONTHS
PEKAH 20	JEHOIAKIM 11
HOSHEA 9	JEHOIACHIN 3 MONTHS
	ZEDEKIAH 11

Captivity: Assyria in 721 B.C.

Captivity: Babylon 70 years.
Jerusalem destroyed in 586 B.C.

5. Prophets of Israel

Israel & Judah:
Micah

Israel (The Ten Tribes):
Hosea, Amos, Obadiah

Judah
(The Two Tribes–Judah & Benjamin):
Isaiah, Jeremiah, Joel, Nahum, Habakkuk, Zephaniah

Exile of Judah:
Ezekiel and Daniel

After the Exile of Judah:
Haggi, Zechariah, Malachi

Nineveh:
Jonah

6. OLD TESTAMENT APOCRYPHA
BOOKS EXCLUDED FROM THE
OLD TESTAMENT CANON

1st Esdras
The retelling of the book of Ezra.

2nd Esdras
Referred to as the Apocalypse of Ezra because of its end-time prophecies.

Tobit
The story of Tobit, who while living in captivity, maintained his righteousness and the practice of his religion.

Judith
This book is more of a suspense story in character, than biblical history.

The additions to Esther
These are chapters that are missing from the Hebrew story of Esther. However, they are included in the Septuagint Version and added at the end of the Vulgate Bible.

The Wisdom of Solomon
More of an intellectual writing, *The Wisdom of Solomon* falls into three parts. In part one thought is given to the afterlife. Part two, a hymn of *Wisdom* as wisdom emanates from God. Part three gives an explanation of the Jewish Exodus.

Ecclesiastticus
Similar to the book of Proverbs, Ecclesiastticus is also known as the Wisdom of Jesus, the Son of Sirach. Sirach handed down the writings of his father to his son, who were both named Jesus. The senior Jesus was known during his time as a wise man among the Hebrews. He wrote words of wisdom and understanding that were widely accepted. His writings and collection of notes from other noble men were arranged in a book by his grandson who incorporated the generations in the book's title.

Baruch
Composed of three sections, history, poetic wisdom and lament, the book of Baruch contains the speeches of Jeremiah.

The Letter of Jeremiah
A short book that warns the exiled Jews against worshipping the idol gods of their captures.

The additions to the Book of Daniel:

The Prayer of Azariah

This prayer is inserted between verses twenty-three and twenty-four of the third chapter of the book of Daniel. Azariah whose Hebrew name is Abednego, was one of the three Hebrew boys thrown into the fiery furnace.

The Song of the Three Young Men

A song of praise by the boys in the fiery furnace follows the prayer to entreat worship to the one true God.

Susanna

Daniel executes his intelligence in finding a loop-hole in the acquisition of adultery against a married woman who refused the sexual advances of two unscrupulous men. This story has its history of use by Shakespeare, the Medieval Church that interpreted the story as the persecuted church and Christ, and Sixteenth and Seventeenth Century artists who illustrated the nudity of the bathing scene in the story.

Bel and the Dragon

The destruction of Bel and the Dragon is another short story of the astuteness of Daniel.

The Prayer of Manasseh

A poetic prayer from the heart of a king who comes to grips with his injurious actions. He realizes that God is merciful and will hear and answer the sincere prayer of repentance.

1ˢᵗ Maccabees

An account of Jewish history that records the expert military skills and strategy of Judah Maccabee (Judas Macabeus), who lead his army to conquest over the Greek dictators of Israel.

2ⁿᵈ Maccabees

The Second Book of Maccabees could have been renamed, as it is not a sequel to the first book. This book tells stories of adhering to the religious practices of Israel during turbulent times, morality and martyrdom.

See chapter five for an explanation of the canonization of the books of the Bible.

NOTES

CHAPTER 4

THE NEW TESTAMENT

The New Testament is a collection of twenty-seven books that bring to life God's Old Testament promise of a redeemer. Each book has its own theme, its own analysis, and its own style, which demonstrates the personality of its authors.

The New Testament books are divided into three groups:

1. The Gospels *"Manifestation"*— Christ is manifested to the world.
2. Acts *"Propagation"*— Christ is preached and His gospel is propagated in the world.
3. The Epistles *"Explanation"*— Christ's gospel is explained.

The book of Revelation is the *"Consummation"*— all the purposes of God in and through Christ are accomplished.

THE SYNOPTIC GOSPELS

The Gospels are of great importance to every believer and great is their influence to those that will be a part of God's Kingdom. They reveal the personality of Jesus Christ and tell the story of His brief life and ministry that was filled with faith and love, as well as His atoning death. *Gospel* signifies good news or glad tidings; the history of Christ's coming into the world and then dying for our sins is indeed good news.

It is assumed that all of the gospels are the same, but this assumption is wrong. The gospels of Matthew, Mark and Luke are similar in their portrayals of the life of Christ, thus they are called *synoptic,* meaning "seeing together." These three gospels parallel the birth, ministry works, crucifixion and resurrection of Christ. However, the writer's personality and targeted audience is different in each.

If we were to compare the gospels of Matthew and Luke, we would find that Matthew was a disciple and eyewitness of the ministry works of Christ, while Luke was not. The public ministry of Christ only extended three and a half years. However, the stories of His birth and childhood are told in the Synoptic Gospels. This being true, an explanation on the accuracy of these gospels is needed. There is a theory that a common document called *Logia,* "Sayings" better known as "Q" was used by these writers (this seems probable even though no such document has ever been found) as well as oral accounts. Just as we've learned in the Old Testament, oral and written references are valid sources in the compilation of the testaments.

Here again, the mind can wonder about the spirituality of these writings, especially if a common document was used. We must remember that the Holy Spirit is always the source of the writings in the Bible making it the "Holy Bible." Because of this, the Bible is not just a collection of poetry, history and letters. It's more than stories about God and His relationship with man. It's not simply a piece of literature that describes man's thoughts and actions. There was divine intervention in the writings of the gospels, which makes them more than ordinary, despite their source or similarities. Inspiration makes each written account unique in its own way.

A common procedure in recording or reenacting a person's life is to find out where that person went, what they did and what they said. By vast opinion, Mark's gospel is probably the oldest gospel. It is conceived that Mark's gospel laid the historical foundation for Matthew and Luke's gospels because it records more of the deeds and actions of Christ.

SURVEY OF THE SYNOPTIC GOSPELS
THE GOSPEL OF MATTHEW

Matthew's gospel is more *Jewish* in nature than the others. It begins with the genealogy of Christ to prove that He was heir to the throne of David and the long awaited *"Messiah"* of the Jews. Contrasting Luke's genealogy, Matthew traces the lineage of Joseph, the father of Christ rather than His mother (who is also in the lineage of David) because the father's lineage was legally recorded.

Matthew 1:16 "And to Jacob was born Joseph the husband of Mary, by whom was born Jesus, who is called Christ."

Matthew reflects upon other matters that would be of more importance to a father. For example:

Virgin Conception[21]

Matthew 1:19–21 "And Joseph her husband, being a righteous man, and not wanting to disgrace her, desired to put her away secretly. But when he had considered this, behold, an angel of the Lord appeared to him in a dream, saying, 'Joseph, son of David, do not be afraid to take Mary as your wife; for that which has been conceived in her is of the Holy Spirit. And she will bear a Son; and you shall call His name Jesus, for it is He who will save His people from their sins.'"

---

21. *In Luke's gospel, the announcement is made to Mary. Luke 1:28.*

Safety

Matthew 2:13 "Now when they had departed, behold, an angel of the Lord appeared to Joseph in a dream, saying, 'Arise and take the Child and His mother, and flee to Egypt, and remain there until I tell you; for Herod is going to search for the Child to destroy Him.'"

Matthew 2:16 "Then when Herod saw that he had been tricked by the magi, he became very enraged, and sent and slew all the male children who were in Bethlehem and in all its environs, from two years old and under, according to the time which he had ascertained from the magi."

Residence

Matthew 2:22–23 "But when he heard that Archelaus was reigning over Judea in place of his father Herod, he was afraid to go there. And being warned by God in a dream, he departed for the regions of Galilee, and came and resided in a city called Nazareth, that what was spoken through the prophets might be fulfilled, 'He shall be called a Nazarene.'"

The Kingdom of Heaven[22] is a major viewpoint in this gospel. Matthew presents Jesus as the "King" the Jews were looking for. Christ's "Sermons on the Mount" in chapter five, is where Christ asserts deity to Himself when He instates the laws and constitutions for His kingdom. The methodical form of the teachings of Christ is a distinguishing characteristic of this gospel.

The Gospel of Mark

Mark, also called John (John being his Jewish name), was the son of one of the Marys in the New Testament, the cousin of Barnabas, and an associate of the apostles Peter and Paul.

As Mark followed Peter, he learned of Jesus whom he hardly knew. Their relationship was so close that Peter referred to Mark as a son. This may explain why the teachings and works of Christ seem to be the reflections of Peter in Mark's gospel.

1st Peter 5:13 "She who is in Babylon, chosen together with you, sends you greetings, and so does my son, Mark."

The Gospel of Mark is particularly fast paced. It, without taking away from the other gospels, portrays a more "action Christ" which resembled Mark's own zealous personality.

Mark's enthusiastic nature caused him to fail in his ministry with the apostle Paul. Becoming more mature, later in several verses of scripture, Mark became very profitable to the apostle's ministry.

---

22. *In the Bible the Kingdom of Heaven and the Kingdom of God are used together. It expresses (a) the sovereign realm and rule of God that is a future state (b) the present state of the Kingdom of God that was manifested by Christ (Matthew 12:28) that is entered into by faith and the new birth (John 3:35).*

Acts 13:13 "Now Paul and his companions put out to sea from Paphos and came to Perga in Pamphylia; and John left them and returned to Jerusalem."

Acts 15:37–38 "And Barnabas was desirous of taking John, called Mark, along with them also. But Paul kept insisting that they should not take him along who had deserted them in Pamphylia and had not gone with them to the work."

Colossians 4:10 "Aristarchus, my fellow prisoner, sends you his greetings; and also Barnabas' cousin Mark (about whom you received instructions: if he comes to you, welcome him)."

2ⁿᵈ Timothy 4:11 "Only Luke is with me. Pick up Mark and bring him with you, for he is useful to me for service."

It seems Mark closely resembles Peter who also made numerous mistakes and blunders as he followed Christ.

Giving a portrait of Jesus as a servant . . . the *"Ideal Worker,"* the Gospel of Mark was written between A.D. 57 and 63. The few references to the Old Testament scriptures, and giving explanations of Jewish words and customs, suggest that this gospel was written especially for the *Romans.* The Romans were more concerned about what Jesus *did* rather than what Jesus *said.* Mark is the shortest gospel, ending in sixteen chapters.

Although Mark's gospel moves you briskly through the activities of Jesus, stimulating the mind with descriptions that draw a picture (as probably Peter's reminiscing put Mark in the scene), it also places emphasis on the periods of rest and prayer taken by Christ; an example for all enthusiastic gospel laborers.

THE GOSPEL OF LUKE

Ancient Christendom (Christianity, followers of Christ, the Church) and New Testament scholars have unanimously ascribed the author of the third gospel to Luke.

Luke who accompanied Paul on many of his missionary trips became a devoted companion, and is referred to as the "beloved physician." The book of Acts, which was also written by Luke, gives further evidence of their closeness.

Colossians 4:14 "Luke, the beloved physician, sends you his greetings, and also Demas."

It is interesting how the family doctor can become a person that is trusted, confided in and very much loved. The relationship is hinged upon the doctor's gentleness, his devotion to his profession and his genuine concern for his patient.

Considering Luke's personality and profession, it stands to reason why his gospel focuses on the gentle side of Christ. Luke being a physician would notice and emphasize the ministry of Jesus to the poor, women, backsliders, the sick and the lost. Christ is portrayed as the compassionate savior whose main concern is healing and restoring life, which is the lifework of a doctor.

Luke, being a learned professional, wrote his gospel appealing to the idealistic mindset of the Greeks portraying Christ as the *"Perfect Man."*

> *Summary of the Synoptic Gospels: We see in the gospels the life of Christ as told by three different evangelists, Matthew, Mark and Luke. Each are successful in presenting the life, character and mission of Jesus Christ. Matthew, a more religious approach to the Jews, proves through genealogy that Jesus was the Messiah. Mark wrote to the methodical Romans and presents Christ as a servant and a redeemer. Lastly, Luke concentrates on the human perfection of Christ to satisfy the Greeks. They've presented "one" Savior for people of every color, culture, intellect, economic class, and religious background. Romans 3:23 "For all have sinned and fall short of the glory of God, being justified as a gift by His grace through the redemption which is in Christ Jesus."*

SURVEY OF ACTS OR THE ACTS OF THE APOSTLES

Luke, the author of the third gospel is undoubtedly the author of the book of Acts. It is unlikely that a different author would write to the same person. If there were such a coincidence, it would be hard to believe that both writers would have the same style. Luke from the very beginning, identifies Acts as his work by his statement to Theophilus where he mentions the "former thesis" which is the Third Gospel.

Acts 1:1 "The first account I composed, Theophilus, about all that Jesus began to do and teach."

Other internal evidence that proves Luke's authorship is in the passages of Scripture where "plurality" is used (Acts 16:10–17; 20:5–15; 21:1–18).

Acts 27:1 "And when it was decided that we should sail for Italy, they proceeded to deliver Paul and some other prisoners to a centurion of the Augustan cohort named Julius."

Acts 28:10 "And they also honored us with many marks of respect; and when we were setting sail, they supplied us with all we needed."

The phrase "we" gives the strong suggestion that the author was an eye-witness to the events that occurred in the book. And since Luke was a traveling companion of Paul, he had first-hand knowledge of the apostle's experiences.

If we compare Luke 24:49 with Acts 1:3–5, Luke gives a hint as to why Acts was written. It is apparent that Luke's latter thesis records what Jesus continued to do and teach through His disciples after they were empowered by the Holy Spirit. In essence, Acts not only records the acts of the apostles, it picks up where the gospels left off.

Luke 24:49 "And behold, I am sending forth the promise of My Father upon you; but you are to stay in the city until you are clothed with power from on high."

Acts 1:3–5 "To these He also presented Himself alive, after His suffering, by many convincing proofs, appearing to them over a period of forty days, and speaking of the things concerning the kingdom of God. And gathering them together, He commanded them not to leave Jerusalem, but to wait for what the Father had promised, 'Which,' He said, 'you heard of from Me; for John baptized with water, but you shall be baptized with the Holy Spirit not many days from now.'"

Acts is one of the most important books in the New Testament because it serves as a bridge that connects the gospels with the continuation of the work of Christ. In the gospels we learn who Christ is and why He came. After His death, burial and resurrection the book of Acts tells us how the gospel of Christ was propagated through the apostles. Acts is the history that gives facts and the background material for the epistles.

The book of Acts also demonstrates Luke's literary ability, and the consecration and dedication of two great apostles, Peter and Paul. It also illustrates the boldness of Stephen and Philip in preaching the gospel.

Finally, there is one very important person revealed in the chapters of the Book of Acts, which without Him, these men would have failed and there would have been no confirmation of the Gospel. This person was the fulfillment of the promise, the power from on high, which fell and changed the course of Bible history as well as the lives of men. This is the time of His administration and His work is not yet completed. He is the continuation of the church that was engineered by Christ. He is the Holy Spirit. Considering these facts, Acts could have very well been titled "The Acts of the Holy Spirit or "Acts of our Glorified Lord."

Acts 2:1–4 "And when the day of Pentecost had come, they were all together in one place. And suddenly there came from heaven a noise like a violent, rushing wind, and it filled the whole house where they were sitting. And there appeared to them tongues as a fire distributing themselves, and they rested on each one of them. And they were all filled with the Holy Spirit and began to speak with other tongues, as the Spirit was giving them utterance."

Acts 10:44–45 "While Peter was still speaking these words, the Holy Spirit fell upon all those who were listening to the message. And all the circumcised believers who had come with Peter were amazed, because the gift of the Holy Spirit had been poured out upon the Gentiles also."

Survey of the Pauline Epistles

Paul was one of the most active missionaries in early church history. As the founder of the churches throughout Asia Minor, Macedonia and Greece, correspondence was necessary to give advice and solve problems within the churches. Having poor eyesight, Paul dictated most of his epistles to a secretary.

Romans 16:22 "I, Tertius, who write this letter, greet you in the Lord."

Galatians 6:11 "See with what large letters I am writing to you with my own hand."

Romans

Paul addresses Judaism, an issue that was prevalent in the Galatian church. In this epistle Paul's approach to the problem is not as hasty as his letter to the Galatians. He addresses the issue by explaining Christianity with a theological approach.

1ˢᵀ CORINTHIANS

The church at Corinth was situated in a bustling commercial city, which fostered many problems. Although a strong church, division, sexual immorality, lawsuits, marriage, offerings to idols were exterior problems for the church. Internal issues such as collection of offerings, church customs and conduct, and even doctrinal beliefs such as the resurrection also existed.

Moreover, the problem of party division demonstrated the carnality of the Corinthian church. Being a party in itself, Christians were competing with the Peterine party—those who were not favorable of Paul but had put aside the Jewish law. A more Judiazing party were the admirers of Apollos. And, there where those who were more devoted to Paul because he was the founder of the church.

Paul addresses all of these issues in sequential order, by divine inspiration and in a few cases, with his own opinion.

1ˢᵗ Corinthians 1:10–13 "Now I exhort you, brethren, by the name of our Lord Jesus Christ, that you all agree, and there be no divisions among you, but you be made complete in the same mind and in the same judgement. For I have been informed concerning you my brethren, by Chloe's people, that there are quarrels among you. Now I mean this, that each one of you is saying, 'I am of Paul,' and 'I of Apollos,' and 'I of Cephas,' and 'I of Christ.' Has Christ been divided? Paul was not crucified for you, was he? Or were you baptized in the name of Paul?"

2ᴺᴰ CORINTHIANS

In this letter Paul expresses what he feels in his heart for the Corinthian church. This time rather than exert his authority as an apostle, he uses the tone of a loving father. Titus brings comfort to Paul by assuring him of the overall census of loyalty to him. Yet he is faced with another problem, the challenge of his apostleship. Throughout the epistle his humility is demonstrated by his faith in God who will provide strength in times of weakness.

2ⁿᵈ Corinthians 11:5–6 "For I consider myself not in the least inferior to the most eminent apostles. But even if I am unskilled in speech, yet I am not so in knowledge; in fact, in every way we have made this evident to you in all things."

2ⁿᵈ Corinthians 12:9–10 "And He has said to me, 'My grace is sufficient for you, for power is perfected in weakness.' Most gladly, therefore, I will rather boast about my weaknesses, that the power of Christ may dwell in me. Therefore I am well content with weaknesses, with insults, with distresses, with persecutions, with difficulties, for Christ's sake; for when I am weak, then I am strong."

GALATIANS

Galatians was written to defend the gospel of free grace from God. The Galatians had become fickle and fallen prey to the judaizing missionaries[23] from Palestine with convincing arguments, which advocated legalism.

The focal point of this letter is "justification by faith." To protect these young converts Paul emphasizes doctrine and gives advice on living a life that is led by the Holy Spirit.

Galatians 1:6 "I am amazed that you are so quickly deserting Him who called you by the grace of Christ, for a different gospel."

EPHESIANS

This epistle addresses no particular problem within the Christian community. It's addressed to the true church, "His Body", all of those in Christ who are everywhere. Written from Rome in A.D. 65, while imprisoned, Paul teaches on God's divine purpose for those who believe in Christ. He also gives procedures on how to live a life conducive to fulfilling that purpose.

Ephesians 4:1–3 "I, Therefore, the prisoner of the Lord, entreat you to walk in a manner worthy of the calling with which you have been called, with all humility and gentleness, with patience, showing forbearance to one another in love, being diligent to preserve the unity of the Spirit in the bond of peace."

PHILIPPIANS

Luke was a former pastor of the Philippian church, which had no apparent problems. By his attention to the church's offerings to meet his needs, Paul expresses love and gratitude to this body of believers. Although a theological presentation of the humility of Christ is given in chapter two, this seems to be a more personal letter.

Philippians 4:15–16 "And you yourselves also know, Philippians, that at the first preaching of the gospel, after I departed from Macedonia, no church shared with me in the matter of giving and receiving but you alone; for even in Thessalonica you sent a gift more than once for my needs."

COLOSSIANS

The news of heresy being generated in this congregation was sent to Paul while he was imprisoned in Rome. Paul immediately addressed the issue. Though he had never visited the church at Colosse, Paul gives warnings to be aware of philosophers with their inciting philosophies. He restates salvation through Jesus Christ without the necessity of ordinances that are weighty and not conducive to the freedom that comes from grace. In this epistle, he also reconfirms the deity of Christ.

Colossians 2:6–8 "As you therefore have received Christ Jesus the Lord,

23. *Judaizers were not Jews; they were Gentiles who over emphasized the Law. Read Galatians 3:15.*

so walk in Him, having been firmly rooted and now being built up in Him and established in your faith, just as you were instructed, and overflowing with gratitude. See to it that no one takes you captive through philosophy and empty deception, according to the tradition of men, according to the elementary principles of the world, rather than according to Christ."

1ST THESSALONIANS

In this epistle, Paul concerns himself with the welfare of the new believers of the church in Thessalonica during a time of persecution. He writes to comfort them by clarifying his teaching on the Second Coming of Christ and warns against pagan influences.

1st Thessalonians 5:23 "Now may the God of peace Himself sanctify you entirely; and may your spirit and soul and body be preserved complete, without blame at the coming of our Lord Jesus Christ."

2ND THESSALONIANS

Written in the same year as 1st Thessalonians, Paul has to readdress the Second Coming of Christ[24]. Waiting on this advent took a literal meaning in the minds of these believers who needed to be charged to work as they waited.

2nd Thessalonians 2:1–2 "Now we request you, brethren, with regard to the coming of our Lord Jesus Christ, and our gathering together to Him, that you may not be quickly shaken from your composure or be disturbed either by a spirit or a message or a letter as if from us, to the effect that the day of the Lord has come."

PHILEMON

In this brief note sent to a runaway slave's master, Paul makes an appeal for forgiveness. Two evangelical pictures are drawn. First we see the concern for the well being of a new convert, and secondly we can picture Christ paying the price for our sins.

Verses 18–19 "But if he has wronged you in any way, or owes you anything, charge that to my account; I, Paul, am writing this with my own hand, I will repay it (lest I should mention to you that you owe to me even your own self as well)."

SURVEY OF THE PASTORAL EPISTLES

Together, these letters can form a spiritual handbook for pastors because they address church organization and worship as well as give instruction and messages of encouragement.

24. *The Second Coming of Christ is also called the Second Advent of Christ. It is when the work of Redemption is completed (John 21:33). It will begin the righteous rule of the Kingdom of God (Romans 19:23, Ephesians 1:14).*

1ST TIMOTHY

Addressed to Timothy a young pastor over the church at Ephesus, Paul gives instructions on the appointment of Bishops and Deacons. He also gives instructions on how to respond to the diverse class of people within the church.

1st Timothy 1:2–4 "To Timothy, my true child in the faith: Grace, mercy and peace from God the Father and Christ Jesus our Lord. As I urge you upon my departure for Macedonia, remain on at Ephesus, in order that you may instruct certain men not to teach strange doctrines, nor to pay attention to myths and endless genealogies, which give rise to mere speculation rather than furthering the administration of God which is by faith."

2ND TIMOTHY

Feeling that his life was about to end, 2nd Timothy seems to be a farewell message to Timothy. Paul reflects on his life and testifies of himself as being a soldier who fought a good fight. As such, he encourages young Timothy to be strong and to remain loyal to the Lord and His truth, despite suffering.

2nd Timothy 2:1–3 "You therefore, my son, be strong in the grace that is in Christ Jesus. And the things which you have heard from me in the presence of many witnesses, these entrust to faithful men, who will be able to teach others also. Suffer hardship with me, as a good soldier of Christ Jesus."

TITUS

Pastor over the Church of Crete, Titus' appointment was equally as strenuous as Timothy's if not more. The church was declining, becoming weak. Again, legalism and mythology began to corrupt the teachings of Christianity. Paul realizes the need to appoint elders and instruct on the duties of older men and women to guide younger believers who would be more susceptible to error.

Titus 1:10–11 "For there are many rebellious men, empty talkers and deceivers, especially those of the circumcision, who must be silenced because they are upsetting whole families, teaching things they should not teach, for the sake of sordid gain."

SURVEY OF THE GENERAL EPISTLES

HEBREWS

Authorship of Hebrews has been ascribed to Paul based on internal evidence. "Better than" is the theme of this epistle. The work of Christ is determined to be "better than" the prophets, angels, Moses, Joshua and Aaron. Further, He is "better than" religious practices and rituals that hindered true faith.

---

24. (continued) *The Second Coming of Christ is to be expected and longed for (Hebrews 9:28, John 14:3). It is a certain event (1st Thessalonians 4:16, Acts 1:11, Revelation 22:12). However, the time of The Second Coming of Christ is unknown (Matthew 24:44, Mark 13:32).*

Hebrews 8:6 "But now He has obtained a more excellent ministry, by as much as He is also the mediator of a better covenant, which has been enacted on better promises."

JAMES

The most Jewish book of the New Testament, the epistle of James brings a more ethical teaching than doctrinal teaching. In the opinion of James, the demonstration of faith is more "works" than religion. James challenges comparison of works and religion. James also provides a series of faith tests[25], which are very useful for Christian ethics.

James 2:17–18 "Even so faith, if it has no works, is dead, being by itself. But someone may well say, 'You have faith, and I have works; show me your faith without the works, and I will show you my faith by my works.'"

1ST PETER

Peter wrote this epistle in A.D. 60 during the burning of Rome by Nero. Hope, conduct and holiness are the apostle's remedy for the suffering of Christians that will eventually give them victory.

1st Peter 4:12-13 "Beloved, do not be surprised at the fiery ordeal among you, which comes upon you for your testing, as though some strange thing were happening to you; but to the degree that you share the sufferings of Christ, keep on rejoicing; so that also at the revelation of His glory, you may rejoice with exultation."

2ND PETER

Peter's second epistle has a much different purpose than the first. Words of encouragement and support under trial and persecution are now followed with warnings against false teachers and their adulterated doctrines.

2nd Peter 2:1-3 "But false prophets also arose among the people, just as there will also be false teachers among you, who will secretly introduce destructive heresies, even denying the Master who bought them, bringing swift destruction upon themselves. And many will follow their sensuality, and because of them the way of the truth will be maligned; and in their greed they will exploit you with false words; their judgement from long ago is not idle, and their destruction is not asleep."

JUDE

This one chapter epistle, written by the brother of Jesus and James, is apocalyptic in nature. Jude does not address any specific group of people within the church, but to the Christian church as a whole, he warns against apostasy.

Verses 21–23 "Keep yourselves in the love of God, waiting anxiously for the mercy of our Lord Jesus Christ to eternal life. And have mercy on some,

---

25. Test of faith 1:1–21. Test of obedience 1:22–25. Test of true religion 1:26–27. Tests of brotherly love 2:1–26. Test of good works 2:14–26. Faith demonstrated by the tongue 3:1–18.

who are doubting; save others, snatching them out of the fire; and on some have mercy with fear, hating even the garment polluted by the flesh."

SURVEY OF THE EPISTLES OF JOHN

THE GOSPEL OF JOHN

John wrote his gospel maintaining that Jesus was the Son of God to refute the Gnostic assertion that He was merely a man. John makes his proof of the deity of Christ theologically in chapter one, verse fourteen. The concept that *The Son of God* was not just another man was supported by the miracles of Christ. John found it necessary to record the miracles of Jesus for further proof of His deity. In John's opinion illustrating the "signs" or miracles performed by Christ, would increase faith in Him and makes eternal life realistic.

John 1:14 "And the Word became flesh, and dwelt among us, and we beheld His glory, glory as of the only begotten from the Father, full of grace and truth."

John 20:30–31 "Many other signs therefore Jesus also performed in the presence of the disciples, which are not written in this book; but these have been written that you may believe that Jesus is the Christ, the Son of God; and that believing you may have life in His name."

In comparison to the Synoptic gospels, John's gospel seems more spiritual than historical. In the Synoptic gospels, Mark writes the reflections of Peter, Luke, as did Paul and Matthew, wrote more like a reporter, systematically recording the facts and teachings of Jesus. Because John was close to Jesus, John's reflections are more intimate thus making his gospel more inspirational.

John outlived the other apostles. Devoted to Christ, he stood with Him before the Sanhedrin and was with Christ at the cross. John was the first to believe in the resurrection. Called the "Son of Thunder," he is affectionately known as the Apostle of Love.

1ST JOHN

Comparing the style and vocabulary of the fourth gospel to 1st John, there is no question that John is the author of this epistle. The aged apostle writes to fellow Christians addressing them as "little children," to assure that salvation is only through Jesus Christ. In this epistle, John paints the picture of a family having a discussion on staying together, loving each other and avoiding outside influences.

1st John 2:12–15 "I am writing to you, little children, because your sins are forgiven you for His name's sake. I am writing to you, fathers, because you know Him who has been from the beginning. I am writing to you, young men, because you have overcome the evil one. I have written to you, children, because you know the Father. I have written to you, fathers, because you know Him who has been from the beginning. I have written to you, young men, because you are strong, and the word of God abides in you, and you have overcome the evil one. Do not love the world, nor the things in the world. If anyone loves the world, the love of the Father is not in him."

2ND JOHN

Addressed to Cyria, "the Elect Lady" who would have been a lady of society, adherence to the truth becomes extremely important to the apostle because of rapid declination brought about by false teachers.

2nd John 10–11 "If anyone comes to you and does not bring this teaching, do not receive him into your house, and do not give him a greeting; for the one who gives him a greeting participates in his evil deeds."

3RD JOHN

Like 2nd John, this epistle is specifically addressed to an individual . . . Gaius, "well beloved." Because of the rise in evangelism, the servants of God and their messages makes hospitality by the church a necessity, contrary to the practice of a church leader who felt otherwise.

3rd John 8–9 "Therefore we ought to support such men, that we may be fellow workers with the truth. I wrote something to the church; but Diotrephes, who loves to be first among them, does not accept what we say."

REVELATION

John, who was exiled to the Isle of Patmos, wrote the apocalyptic book of the New Testament, Revelation. Revelation was written to give hope and cheer to Christians who were undergoing great persecution.

Revelation 1:3 "Blessed is he who reads and those who hear the words of the prophecy, and heed the things which are written in it; for the time is near."

Revelation contains many symbols, signs and visions that can be easily misinterpreted. Many Bible scholars steer clear of making affirmation of their interpretations which can be lead to "adding or deleting" from the prophecy, something that is strongly warned against. Reading this book however, is strongly suggested. Regardless of its judgements and dooms, Jesus is glorified and the believer is blessed with victory forever. Revelation is a fitting ending to what began so beautifully in the book of Genesis.

Revelation 21:1–4 "And I saw a new heaven and a new earth; for the first heaven and the first earth passed away, and there is no longer any sea. And I saw the holy city, new Jerusalem, coming down out of heaven from God, made ready as a bride adorned for her husband. And I heard a loud voice from the throne, saying, 'Behold, the tabernacle of God is among men, and He shall dwell among them, and they shall be His people, and God Himself shall be among them, and He shall wipe away every tear from their eyes; and there shall no longer be any death; there shall no longer be any mourning, or crying, or pain; the first things have passed away.'" ❖

CHAPTER 5

FORMATION OF THE BIBLE

Canon is the term used to identify books to be included in the Bible based on their inspirational content. Taken from the Greek word "kanon," (which means rule or standard), the books of the Old and New Testaments of the Christian Bible are recognized as being authoritative. The books that are excluded are called the Apocrypha (meaning hidden, see chart on page 27). Although the books of the Apocrypha can be valued for its variety of literary content, the early church did not recognize them because they lacked divine inspiration.

Testament derives from the Greek word *"covenant"* or *"will"* and from the Latin translation *"testamentum."* In the Bible, covenants are agreements between God and man, which were meant to foster a closer relationship with Him. Although there are two testaments in the Bible, they are not entirely separate since one concludes the other. The Old Testament, which is historical in nature, conveys the promises of God concerning salvation for His people, while the New Testament fulfills that promise.

From the time of man's fall, God made promises to provide him with salvation, which included prosperity. The Old Testament gives numerous accounts of man's struggle and failure to maintain a moral and spiritual relationship with his Creator, which made the fulfillment of those promises desperately longed for. In the New Testament, the promises of God were finally attained through Jesus Christ who brought salvation to man, which transformed hope into a reality. Hence, the "new covenant" is better than the "old covenant."

Genesis 3:15 "'And I will put enmity between you and the woman, And between your seed and her seed; He shall bruise you on the head, And you shall bruise him on the heel.'"

Exodus 24:8 "So Moses took the blood and sprinkled it on the people, and said, 'Behold the blood of the covenant, which the LORD has made with you in accordance with all these words.'"

Jeremiah 31:31 "'Behold days are coming,' declares the LORD, 'when I will make a new covenant with the house of Israel and with the house of Judah.'"

1st Corinthians 11:25 "In the same way He took the cup also, after supper, saying, 'This cup is the new covenant in My blood; do this, as often as you drink it, in remembrance of Me.'"

The books of the Bible are much more than history, poetry, legend and revelation. God's Word sets the standard for righteous living and gives guidelines for moral behavior. What God has planned and wills for His people are discovered in the pages of His written Word. Who and what to believe, how to worship, faith and true forms of religion are all revelations from God. Revealed to us by inspiration, God's Word is authoritative and established forever.

Mark 13:31 "Heaven and earth will pass away, but My words will not pass away."

The use of godly men was necessary to determine which books would be canonized as the Bible, the authoritative Word of God. These men were heads of various Christian churches known as "Councils." The human effort to incorporate the volumes of the Bible was assisted by the Spirit of God who inspired these men in their decisions. Hence, the compilation of the books is less human and more divine. The providence of God through divine revelation and inspiration, in the canonizing of the Bible takes precedence over the human element.

THE OLD TESTAMENT FORMATION

The actual formation of the Hebrew Bible cannot be traced. It is speculated that the three divisions of the Hebrew Bible may be the order in which they were received.

The Pentateuch is first to appear in the Hebrew Bible as it was considered the *Law* of God to be observed by His people.

Deuteronomy 31:24–26 "And it came about, when Moses finished writing the words of this law in a book until they were complete, that Moses commanded the Levites who carried the ark of the covenant of the LORD, saying, 'Take this book of the law and place it beside the ark of the covenant of the LORD your God, that it may remain there as a witness against you.'"

Given the level of inspiration and acceptance as "divine messages" from God, the Prophetical books appear second. Held with the same regard, are the books that comprise The Writings, which appear third. Tradition has it that Ezra was the first to accomplish canonizing these books. In approximately 90 A.D., at the Council of Jamnia, the Scriptures of the Hebrew Bible was formally accepted as we have them today . . . The Old Testament.

NEW TESTAMENT FORMATION

The Bible of the early church was the Old Testament, which became somewhat of a missionary Bible. During the Apostolic age of the church, the New Testament writings that contained divine revelation and inspiration, were also acknowledged as having divine authority. Because of this authority, they were read in public meetings along with the Old Testament.

1st Thessalonians 5:27 "I adjure you by the Lord to have this letter read to all the brethren."

The New Testament began its formation with the missionary letters of the Apostle Paul. Paul's letters, because of his concern for the church at Thessalonica, contributed the first book of the New Testament—1st Thessalonians. A second letter, 2nd Thessalonians followed a few months later.

During his third missionary journey, letters were written to the Corinthian (1st and 2nd Corinthians), Galatian and Roman churches. While in prison, Paul wrote what are called the "Prison Epistles"—Philippians, Philemon, Colossians and Ephesians. Afterward, letters to Timothy (1st and 2nd Timothy) and Titus, known as the "Pastoral Epistles" appeared.

Mark was the first of the Gospels to emerge. The Gospel of Matthew soon followed then the Gospel of Luke. The Book of Acts, which gives a narration of the continued work of Christ through the Holy Spirit and the expansion of the church soon surfaced. Then the Book of Hebrews appeared to stabilize Christians who were contemplating returning to Judaism.

The Universal writings—1st and 2nd Peter, James and Jude were circulated at the time of Paul's letters. These books, also called the Apostle's Creed, General or Catholic Epistles, were not addressed to any specific church, but to the church as a whole.

The last of the New Testament writings to appear—The Gospel of John, 1st, 2nd and 3rd John and Revelation—were written by the Apostle John.

At the end of the first century, all of the writings of the New Testament were in circulation. However, the church did not have these authoritative writings as we do today in one collection. This is supported by Paul's instruction to the Colossians to share his letter with the Laodiceans.

Colossians 4:16 "And when this letter is read among you, have it also read in the church of the Laodiceans; and you, for your part read my letter that is coming from Laodicea."

This eventually led to the embodiment of all the letters of Paul in one collection. Next came the collection of the Gospels. Revelation was circulated by itself, and then Acts which was placed with the Gospels in some manuscripts of the New Testament, and in others, placed with the Universal Epistles.

Through the centuries that followed, various canons of the New Testament were formed that included the New Testament Apocrypha. The list changed many times as the Councils added and deleted from the so-called "official" canon. In 397, the council of Carthage gave its official statement asserting the present twenty-seven books as the New Testament Scriptures.

Considering that the Bible is divine revelation and that the writers were all inspired by the Holy Spirit, it can be conceived that God made the finalization of the Canon. If we trust in the authority of the contents of the Bible, then that trust should be extended to its formation.

John 16:13–15 "But when He, the Spirit of truth, comes, He will guide you into all the truth; for He will not speak on His own initiative, but whatever He hears, He will speak; and He will disclose to you what is to come. He shall glorify Me; for He shall take of Mine, and shall disclose it to you."❖

CHAPTER 6

TRANSLATIONS OF THE BIBLE

EARLY TRANSLATIONS

Because of its universal message and divine purpose, the Old and New Testaments have been translated either together or as separate volumes, into several languages. The most common are as follows:

Samaritan Pentateuch
As described in its name, the Samaritan Pentateuch only consists of the books of the Law. Although considered canonized by the Samaritans in Palestine, the Samaritan Pentateuch differs from the accepted or "received" traditional Jewish canon.

Masoretic Text
The Old Testament was translated by a group of Rabbis of Tiberias and Babylon who were called Masoretes. They considered their translation correct and complete, thus bearing their name to distinguish it from the others.

The Aramaic Translation
Arabic became the language of the Jews who returned to Palestine from Babylonian exile in 536 B.C. making this translation from the Hebrew text very necessary.

The Targums
To explain the Hebrew text, they were paraphrased in the Aramaic tongue. Eventually the oral translations of the Old Testament were written and compiled into what is known as the Aramaic Targums.

Septuagint (LXX)
The Greek translation of the Old Testament is called the Septuagint, one of the oldest translations of the Hebrew Bible. It was used by Jesus, the apostles, the early church and it is quoted in the New Testament. The translation's name is Latin meaning "seventy" which correlates with the legend ascribing the work to seventy-two elders.

Vulgate
Damascus, the Bishop of Rome, commissioned Jerome to revise the Latin Bible. The Vulgate became the only recognized authoritative Bible of Western Europe in 382.

The Ethiopic Version

An Ethiopian sect called Jewish falasha (African Jews) made use of this Bible translation which contained several of the apocryphal books. They claimed to have been descendants of Hebrew immigrants during the time of King Solomon and Queen Sheba.

The Coptic Version

Called the Egyptian Coptic version, this translation from the Hebrew Bible took place at the same time as the Septuagint translation.

ENGLISH TRANSLATIONS OF THE BIBLE

Wycliffe Bible

For many years the only Bible that was available for Christians was the Latin Vulgate, made by Jerome between A.D. 383 and 405. Clergymen and the monks were the only people who could read the Latin Vulgate, as they were the only ones who were familiar with the language. The Oxford theologian, John Wycliffe, translated the Bible in the language of the laymen, which was a revolutionary idea at the time. He was a vital part of the Reformation and held strongly to the belief that the way to defeat Rome was to make the Bible readily available to everyday people for their own understanding.

Tyndale's Bible

William Tyndale greatly influenced the progress of translating the Bible into English. His desire to make the Bible available to all was not peacefully accepted by the Catholic Church, or the Bishop of London. As a result Tyndale spent much of his time translating hiding and fleeing. Eventually he was strangled and his body was burned at the stake for his work. In 1525, 3000 copies of the New Testament were published. Although persecuted for his translation, 90% of Tyndale's work is replicated in the King James Version. Tyndale was killed before he completed his translation of the Old Testament. Tyndale's work and death aided in creating a desire for the Bible in English, and the government eventually saw the necessity in having the Bible available for lay people.

Coverdale's Bible

In 1535, while Tyndale was jailed for his translation, Miles Coverdale completed the first English printed Bible. His version was translated in German and Latin. Two new editions of his Bible were completed with the King of England's sanction, who less than a year before killed Tyndale for his work.

Matthew's Bible

Matthew's Bible is the first complete Bible in the English language, which was actually printed in England. The entire New Testament and half of the Old Testament was from the work of Tyndale, while the remainder was the translations of Coverdale. On the title page "Set forth with the king's most gracious license" appears, indicating the support and blessing of the English government.

The Great Bible

The next Bible to appear in England was completed by Coverdale. It was actually a revision of the Matthew Bible. After this Bible was circulated no new translations of the Bible were done. During this time much emphasis was placed on the importance of reading the Bible, and printing the existing versions. King Edward VI demanded by court order that the Great Bible be placed in every parish church.

The Genevan Bible/Breeches Bible

William Whittingham, brother in law of the great Protestant leader John Calvin, revised the next English Bible. While in Geneva escaping martyrdom and persecution under Queen Mary, he revised the English New Testament with verse divisions, and printed it in Roman type in 1557. In 1560 he and his associates produced a revision of the whole Bible. It was highly popular and underwent 160 editions. Its popularity continued after the publication of the King James Version in 1611.

The Bishop's Bible

During the reign of Queen Elizabeth the decree of Edward VI was reinstated and a copy of the Great Bible was again in every church. With the Genevan Bible in circulation the discrepancies and shortcomings of the Great Bible became more evident. Archbishop Parker and eight other bishops undertook the task of revising the Great Bible. This work was completed in 1568 and was known as the Bishop's Bible. Although it was relatively popular it did not supercede the popularity of the Genevan Bible.

King James Version

The King James Version is the most popular version for English speaking Protestant Christians, in both the public and private arenas. This version has been around for more than 350 years. It took two years to complete, and after the completion nine months were dedicated to revising the revision. Much of the reason this translation has withstood time as the most popular translation is due to the thorough translation process.

When King James assumed the throne of England in 1603, he authorized a new translation of the Bishop's Bible. Instead of one man or a small group of men working on the translation, forty-seven of the best Hebrew and Greek scholars were commissioned for the task. Some were responsible for the Old Testament, New Testament and the Apocrypha and after a group finished a section of translation another group of men reviewed it. There was a great system of checks and balances and a consensus had to be reached on questionable passages or words.

In 1611 the King James Version was completed and did not immediately receive rave reviews. In fact it took over 50 years for it to replace the Genevan Bible in popularity. Over the course of time minor changes have been made to spelling, and word usage but no major revisions have been done to the King James Version.

English Revised Version

Over the course of time, the language of the King James Version became obsolete and Greek translations that were superior to those that were available to King James translators became available. These two factors were the underlying cause for the English Revised Version of the Bible. Two companies with 27 men each for the Old Testament and New Testament were employed to revise the King James Version, with the Convocation of Canterbury of the Church of England in 1870. In their translations the team found numerous differences, but none that affected the doctrines of the Bible.

This version received great instant popularity, with 3 million copies sold in its first year of publication. However, it has not been considered a work with unparalleled supremacy.

American Standard Version

The American Standard Version, published in 1901, was the product of American revisers who worked on the English Revised Version. This group of scholars regarded some of the language in the English Revised Version as antiquated and obsolete. They also came across many words that were English but not necessarily American in their meanings and usage. For American use, it is considered to be superior to the English Revised Version.

Twentieth Century Versions

In the late 19th century archeologists discovered Greek writings in Egyptian deserts. These writings used the everyday Greek language of the people. The Greek was not classical or formal, but common speech. This brought about a desire to have the Bible in the everyday language of people, as opposed to the classical and formal English. As a result many new translations began to appear. Individuals completed some of the newer versions and others were completed by committees and commissioned by Christian organizations. ❖

NOTES

CHAPTER 7

SUPPLEMENT

EARLY WRITING MATERIALS

STONE

The earliest writing material used in Egypt, Babylon and Palestine was stone.

Exodus 31:18 "And when He had finished speaking with him upon Mount Sinai, He gave Moses the two tablets of the testimony, tablets of stone, written by the finger of God."

WOOD

Usually in the form of tablets, wood was used in Greece, Egypt and Palestine during ancient times.

Habakkuk 2:2 "Then the LORD answered me and said, 'Record the vision and inscribe it on tablets, That the one who reads it may run.'"

PAPYRUS

Because of its abundance, papyrus was one of the most resourceful writing materials during ancient times. The Nile River was the source of papyrus, which became the common writing material for Egypt, Greece and Rome. Production of papyrus (the paper of Biblical times) required proficient skill. Thin cuts from the stem were joined together to form the first layer. A second moistened layer was then pressed across the first. The sheet was then dried and polished. Rolls of papyrus were made by joining several sheets together. The New Testament writings were written on papyrus. For convenience, these writings were put together in book form, which is known as the "papyrus codex."

VELLUM/PARCHMENT

It was customary to use animal skin as writing material during Biblical times. Unlike ordinary leather or hide, vellum/parchment suggested a finer quality of writing material. Vellum relates to the English word "veal," which may have been either calf or antelope skins. Parchment indicated the use of sheep or goat skins. Copies of the New Testament writings on vellum or parchment existed for more than a thousand years. As with papyrus, the process required master level skills.

2nd Timothy 4:13 "When you come bring the cloak which I left at Troas with Carpus, and the books, especially the parchments."

PAPER

Being the first to practice and produce paper, the Chinese who were cap-tured by Arabs in the mid-eighth century, made this new writing material known. By the thirteenth century, paper became the modern and more prominent writing material in Europe.

WRITING TOOLS

STYLUS

A sharp instrument used on clay or wax materials. An iron stylus was used as an engraving tool on stone.

Job 19:23–24 "Oh that my words were written! Oh that they were inscribed in a book! That with an iron stylus and lead they were engraved in the rock forever!"

Jeremiah 17:1 "The sin of Judah is written down with an iron stylus; With a diamond point it is engraved upon the tablet of their heart, And on the horns of their altars."

REED

Made from wood a reed was used as a pen to write on papyrus or paper.

3 John 13-14 "I had many things to write to you, but I am not willing to write them to you with pen and ink; but I hope to see you shortly, and we shall speak face to face. Peace be to you. The friends greet you. Greet the friends by name."

INTERPRETATION OF SCRIPTURES

Bible Context is a method used to assist in achieving an effective meaning to a passage of scripture. There are four principles to this method of Bible study for a better understanding of the scriptures.

Principal Context – used when scripture is studied so as to shed light on a particular subject, thing or concept. In this principal, the scriptures that proceed as well as follow the subject matter must be studied in the light of its context.

Near Context – is applied to help clarify some of the hard to understand scriptures by cross-referencing them with other scriptures. Even when this is done, the reader may assume their implication.

Remote Context – involves the use of reference books, Bible dictionaries and commentaries, as well as other translations of the Bible. This method is most useful when a particular passage of scripture seems obscure or vague.

Application Context – is what proceeds the achievement of correct interpretation of the passage of scripture being studied. After discovering its truth, the scripture can then be applied, in some cases more than once. It is possible to have several applications, but there can only be one interpretation.

BIBLE TEXT

Progression of Scripture – progression is the method used by God who makes a revelation or truth clear. God's Word moves progressively until it reaches its culmination or its consummation.

Genesis 3:15 "And I will put enmity Between you and the woman, And between your seed and her seed; He shall bruise you on the head, And you shall bruise him on the heel."

> *(Genesis 12:3; Deuteronomy 18:15; Psalms 22; Jeremiah*
> *23:5, Ezekiel 17:22; Daniel 2:34; Micah 5:2; Haggai 2:7;*
> *Zechariah 3:8; Malachi 3:1)*

Matthew 1:18-21 "Now the birth of Jesus Christ was as follows. When His mother Mary had been betrothed to Joseph, before they came together she was found to be with child by the Holy Spirit. And Joseph her husband, being a righteous man, and not wanting to disgrace her, desired to put her away secretly. But when he had considered this, behold, an angel of the Lord appeared to him in a dream, saying, 'Joseph, son of David, do not be afraid to take Mary as your wife; for that which has been conceived in her is of the Holy Spirit. And she will bear a Son; and you shall call His name Jesus, for it is He who will save His people from their sins.'"

> *(Matthew 1:22; Luke 21:22; John 12:38; Acts 3:18)*

Discontinuity in Scripture – gaps are discovered more frequently in the Old Testament rather than the New Testament. In Jewish scripture, omission of specific dates, time frames or large periods of time is common without explanation. In most cases, these omissions go unnoticed.

Textural Criticism – has two sides, higher and lower. Higher criticism deals with the authorship, history, dates, places, internal and external evidence contained in scripture. Lower criticism focuses on critiquing the text itself. Biblical manuscripts were copied several times in several different languages by human hands, which explains why mistakes are found. Misinterpretation of words, misunderstanding of languages being translated and omission of words are frequent but unintentional. Human error in translation has a minor effect on the accuracy of Biblical text.

WRITING STYLES

Uncial Capital letters was a writing style in straight columns that omitted spacing between words and prouncuation. There are approximately 375 uncial manuscripts in existence; the most popular uncials are the Vatican, Sinaitic and Alexandrian.

THEREFOREHAVINGBEENJUST	TRIBULATIONSKNOWINGTHA
IFIEDBYFAITHWEHAVEPEACE	TTRIBULTIONBRINGSABOUTPE
WITHGODTHROUGHOURLOR	RSEVERANCEANDPERSEVERA
DJESUSCHRISTTHROUGHWHO	NCEPROVENCHARACTERAND
MALSOWEHAVEOBTAINEDOU	PROVENCHARACTERHOPEAN
RINTRODUCTIONBYFAITHINT	DHOPEDOESNOTDISAPPOINT
OTHISGRACEINWHICHWESTA	BECAUSETHELOVEOFGODHAS
NDANDWEEXULTINHOPEOTH	BEENPOUREDOUTWITHINOUR
EGLORYOFGODANDNOTONLY	HEARTSTHROUGHTHEHOLYSP
THISBUTWEALSOEXULTINOUR	IRITWHOWASGIVENTOUS

Example of Romans 5:1-5

Cursive was a smaller free-hand writing style, which made up the majority of the 5000 manuscripts of the New Testament. This style of writing appeared during the ninth century. The cursive writing closely resembles today's script handwriting.

ARCHEOLOGY AND THE BIBLE

The discovery of ancient artifacts that were found in the deserts, caves and buried cities of Biblical times are helpful in certifying some of the stories that are in the Bible. The archeological finds of pottery played an important role in identifying the various races, lifestyles and cultures of the people of that period. The climate of many Bible regions made the preservation of writings on clay tablets and papyrus available for discovery of the many different languages, traditions and religious practices of ancient civilizations.

Archeological Manuscript Discoveries

Papyrus – Bible text found in Egypt.

Clay Tablets – literature found in the regions of Mesopotamia and Syria that identify several different languages and dialogues.

Ugarit Tablets – define the Canaanite dialect that closely resembles ancient Hebrew.

Hellenistic Manuscripts – aid in the understanding of their focus of the New Testament text.

The Dead Sea Scrolls – written by the men of Qumran, the scrolls not only supplies us with text used during the times of Christ, they give us the religious transfer of the Old Testament to the New, and the history of Judaism to the rise of Christianity.

Although archeology plays an important role in Bible history, it is not intended to prove the validity of the written Word of God. Rather than prove, archeology *supports* the Word of God. The finding of ancient materials dismisses the notion that the Bible is mere legend, fable and imagination. Archaeology gives a historical framework for the actual events that occurred thousands of years ago. Archeological finds substantiates the reality of an invisible God who interacts with His creation to become known.❖

In this series:

Volume 1: Introduction to Bible Doctrine
*A Systematic Study of Seven Doctrines of the
Christian Faith* — Made Easy

Volume 2: Introduction to Bible Origin
A Study of the Formation of the Bible

Volume 3: Introduction to Typology and Symbolism
*An Expository Study of Types and Symbols
Found in the Bible*

To order Bulk Volumes for Bible Study Groups go to:
www.swalkerpublications.com

To receive credit toward a Certificate in Biblical Studies for this
series, send your request to: itmt@theinstituteoftheology.org

Attend Bible College at HOME!
The Institute of Theology and Ministry Training go to:
www.theinstituteoftheology.org

Made in the USA
Lexington, KY
15 September 2019